Pebble™

Communities

Living in a
Rural Area

by Lisa Trumbauer

Consulting Editor: Gail Saunders-Smith, PhD

Capstone
press
Mankato, Minnesota

Pebble Books are published by Capstone Press,
151 Good Counsel Drive, P.O. Box 669, Mankato, Minnesota 56002.
www.capstonepress.com

1 2 3 4 5 6 10 09 08 07 06 05

Library of Congress Cataloging-in-Publication Data
Trumbauer, Lisa, 1963–
    Living in a rural area / by Lisa Trumbauer.
    p. cm.—(Communities)
    Includes bibliographical references and index.
    ISBN 0-7368-3631-4 (hardcover)
    1. Country life. I. Title. II. Communities (Mankato, Minn.)
GT3470.T78 2005
307.72—dc22   2004011161

Summary: Simple text and photographs describe life in rural areas.

Note to Parents and Teachers

The Communities set supports social studies standards related
to people, places, and geography. This book describes and
illustrates life in rural areas. The images support early readers in
understanding the text. The repetition of words and phrases helps
early readers learn new words. This book also introduces early
readers to subject-specific vocabulary words, which are defined in
the Glossary section. Early readers may need assistance to read
some words and to use the Table of Contents, Glossary, Read More,
Internet Sites, and Index sections of the book.

Table of Contents

Rural Areas

A rural area
is a type of community.
A rural area
is in the country.

A rural area
can be near an ocean.
A rural area
can be in a desert.

A rural area
has open space.
People in a rural area
live in houses
that are far apart.

In a rural area,
people go a long way
to buy things they need.
They travel to stores
and places to eat.

Work in a Rural Area

A rural area
may have farms.
Farmers grow crops
for people and animals
to eat.

A rural area
may have ranches.
Many ranchers
raise cattle.

Some people
in a rural area
work from their homes.

Fun in a Rural Area

Some people
in a rural area
ride snowmobiles.

In a rural area,
relatives often live nearby.
Do you live
in a rural area?

Glossary

community—a group of people who live in the same area

country—land that is away from towns or cities

crop—a plant grown in large amounts; corn, wheat, and potatoes are crops.

desert—a dry area of land with few plants; deserts receive very little rain.

ocean—a large body of water

ranch—a large farm for horses, sheep, or cattle

rancher—a person who works on a ranch

snowmobile—a vehicle with an engine and skis; snowmobiles travel on snow.

Read More

Francis, Sandy. *At the Farm.* Field Trips. Chanhassen, Minn.: Child's World, 2000.

Holland, Gini. *I Live in the Country.* Where I Live. Milwaukee: Weekly Reader Early Learning Library, 2004.

Miller, Jake. *Who's Who in a Rural Community.* Communities at Work. New York: PowerKids Press, 2005.

Internet Sites

FactHound offers a safe, fun way to find Internet sites related to this book. All of the sites on FactHound have been researched by our staff.

Here's how:

1. Visit *www.facthound.com*
2. Type in this special code **0736836314** for age-appropriate sites. Or enter a search word related to this book for a more general search.
3. Click on the **Fetch It** button.

FactHound will fetch the best sites for you!

Index

Word Count: 129
Grade: 1
Early-Intervention Level: 13

Editorial Credits
Mari C. Schuh, editor; Kate Opseth, designer; Jo Miller, photo researcher; Scott Thoms, photo editor

Photo Credits
BananaStock Ltd., cover (girl)
Bruce Coleman Inc./George Rockwin, 8; John Elk III, 4; Julie Eggers, 14
Capstone Press/Gary Sundermeyer, 18
Corbis/Royalty Free, 1
Digital Vision, cover (background), 16
Getty Images/Andy Sacks, 20
Index Stock Imagery/Greig Cranna, 6
OneBlueShoe, 10
Pat & Chuck Blackley, 12